Water of Joy

poems by

Mike Matthews

Finishing Line Press
Georgetown, Kentucky

Water of Joy

ACKNOWLEDGMENTS

I would like to say thank you to the monks in Huánggāng for inviting me for tea
and giving me a place to rest within serenity. Thank you Master Chóng Dì, my
friend Sunshine (Shèngxuán), my friend Zhāng Yì. I learned that breathing,
smiling, drinking tea, and discussing poetry differ not in the slightest. Also,
thank you to Wáng Lèkāng in Běijīng for thoroughly understanding these
poems. Your deep understanding encouraged me greatly.

Thank you to my supporting friends in the writing groups for kick-starting
me to get this done and to those who let me try these poems in readings to
see if they would fly.

Thank you to my wife, Huī Qín, for noticing my idle times and gently
encouraging me to get to work on my poetry.

Thank you to the editors of the journal, *When it rains from the ground up*, for
published my poem, "Mahamudra Pancakes," so long ago.

Publisher: Leah Maines
Editor: Christen Kincaid
Cover Art: Mike Matthews
Author Photo: Nicole M. Metts
Cover Design: Elizabeth Maines McCleavy

Printed in the USA on acid-free paper.
Order online: www.finishinglinepress.com
also available on amazon.com

Author inquiries and mail orders:
Finishing Line Press
P. O. Box 1626
Georgetown, Kentucky 40324
U. S. A.

Table of Contents

Before Sunrise

The sphere of light from the lamppost
diffused by misty fog
holds back the encroaching dark night.

The roads at the intersection
extend into emptiness.

The sky shows no stars.

Soon, the sun will shake away the fog,
and the morning will outshine the lamplight.

Then stop signs, busy traffic,
rough engines, and car horns
will define the outlines of the streets.

The lamppost's thick glass fixture
hangs on impermanent red and green wires.
It will fall soon, and the bulb will break.

Then the night will encompass the lamppost
and everything within its small light.

Before the sunrise, before the new light,
the stillness of the silence and the dark
will define no objects, no street to travel.

The shape of nothing will appear
as the endless form of serenity.

Dreambirds

Nighthawks rarely touch ground
preferring to swing through moonlight
to part thick darkness with their crazy
screeching and sharp dicing wings.

To them the dark is water. Their wings
stir the liquid soft-light of moon.

Once, so small, one bird stood lightly
at the edge of the light circle of the streetlamp—
simple, perfect bird, color of the moon.

Then the night picked up the bird
like the drop of a dream, light like a dream,
soft light dreaming in drops of birds.

For Tomorrow Morning

Expect of me the access of my hour.

I'll wait to meet myself when light moves slowly,
when I'm a still moth drying my wings.

Hook a portrait to my profile,
and sling a critique onto my contrasts.

I'll reflect opposites of me
that I might have a look at my asymmetric face.

Leave me a list next to my shallow dreams
so that I can march through them like an instinct.

My shoes will have to anticipate my return
if they have not shrunk from thirst already.

Spray your graffiti onto my forehead with a kiss
when I'm a blurry bed cover.

I'll diffuse in the erratic strings of sunlight on water
when I lose my grip on my breath and submerge
                    into the dark blue of dissolution.

Behind Me, the Rain

The rain behind me,
outside the window,
softly plays through the leaves,
dances lightly on the grass
and on the porch.

I breathe the rhythm of the rain
and try to trust my back
to steady me upright
against the distant thunder.

In the stillness of the storm,
a train's horn
announces thoughts
traveling from the past
almost forgotten.

I Walked in the Rain

Damp, cold arms…
Rain pecks the brim of my hat,
the wet lawns, the sidewalk—
all sound with all notes
of all music sing each drop.

The cold reminds me
that I am here. I've turned
inward where the leaves have gone.

I approach the timelessness of breath
when brilliance overcomes the mind
and passing trains and someone coughing
unify a senseless pattern of blended
conversations, all moving through me
without scratching the wind.

I reach for a piece of that sun
that silently filters through glass and air,
and I feel as small as the drop in my palm,
as large as the star's shell filling me
in a black chair.

Open, opened, nothing…
No more names for colors
of the sunset in boxes
of organized wires of nerves.
The look of motion, my torso
bends, body moves, muscles
cross rocky land. Liquids
pump like the undulations of worms,
like birds crying between rock
and sand, and my hands open and close
like jellyfish in waves
that break against cliffs that fall.

Night Rain

Night rained under the umbrella.
Your back soaked through your dress.

On our walk to our apartment,
bricks of the sidewalk floated

like carnival toy boats
pushed under our feet.

All the taxis passed with red signs:
"Yôu kè," "Zài kè," full of passengers.

The roads churned, grey-black rivers
with bottomless puddles under each curb.

"If we walk across China," I said, "to go visit England,
we will be prepared for many rainstorms."

Wet feet will never steal my laughter
whenever I walk in a downpour with you.

Hooked in Water

There is a lake,
        always a lake.
There is a tree,
        always a tree.

There is someone fishing,
        and fishing, and fishing,

sitting very still
with a simple pole,
one line in the water.

I rest in the water
pierced by the hook

waiting for the fish to be hungry.

Between Air and Water

Today I breathe
between air and water.

I breathe into the water,
Out, 2, 3…
I turn and breathe in the air.

I breathe into the water,
Out, 2, 3…
I turn and breathe in the air.

Tiny blue square tiles
mark distance like frames
around random instances.

The tiles form a long letter I.

I glide between air and water,
neither forward nor backward.

The air pressure pushes me down.
The water pressure holds me up.

The line between air and water
shines like a ribbon of silver.

I am between water and air
like I am between birth and death,
gliding along the silver line,

breathing in the air
and transferring air
to the water,

breathing out the air
and transferring water
to the air.

I turn and swim, turn and swim,
each stroke along the long letter I.

No beginning, no end.

Bardo Bus

On the bus,
in the belly of the hound,
we carried karmic luggage
from the end of one life
into the beginning of the next.

At each stop,
there was no music,
no chant, no mantra,
no form, no emptiness,
no eye, no ear, no nose,
no emptiness of form

to guide us through
the middle, the Bardo.

There were migraines
and rain and lightening bolts
and a general gloom

weighing us down, passengers,
weighing down our shoulders,
weight from our past lives
no matter the sorrow or the joy.

There were short breaks—
five minutes to get medicine
to stay the throbbing temple.

No one spoke
while riding between our recent pasts
and our veiled futures.

When the doors split opened,
each of us entered a new life,
carrying the intangible weight
of the one we left hours before.

Layers of Dirt

We throw dirt
on the natural spirit within

and see the dirt
as what we think is real.

Underneath the layers
that cloak simple love

is a spirit like a butterfly
with amethyst wings.

You stretched your wings
with your name like the light

and started a hurricane in my chest
that has blown away the dirt

so that I can be the spirit
who sweeps the steps of the temple

to uncover and uncover
the natural love for you.

I Don't Know Because I Sit among the Air

Amorphous and amphibious,
I breathe lightly detached from effort
water and air alike, no lines between
vapor and tree, stone and cloud.

Like the shape of an eyeball of glass
peaking over the peak of a cloud
above a mountain, I cross my legs
and fail to define the forest,
though chipmunks hesitantly approach
and then skitter off like little boats
with sails of tortillas flapping in the wind!

The Mind's Job

The mind manufactures thoughts steadily
like lungs transfer oxygen molecules into blood.
Healthy organs function well without supervision.

Thoughts entertain any kind of reality—
The job of the organ of the mind!

Inside that reality lives so much to do,
like rearranging so many possible outcomes
inside a virtual cave full of thin colorful shadows—
So comfortable it must be in there!

Yet, the boundaries of the swirling realities
that appear solid gently part like thin wind
the moment one releases the mind
to do its job on its own without attention.

When the vapor walls part,
the space outside the mind's noise
floats so lightly and violet like weightless breath.

Vapored Thoughts

Thoughtlessness:
Bubbles in a hot tub,
my mind mildly melts.

My eyelids lightly close.

Jet streams cut away
layers of my ego
until nothing important
remains but a vapor.

Walking Breath
for Sunshine

Though I walk and I notice
when one foot leaves
the ground, when the other
first touches, and the wind shifts
with each circle I complete
around the tower, and I hear
the birdsong's crescendo
and diminuendo with each turn,
my breath stays in front of me,
or gets lost in the city
honking its horns beyond
the temple's walls.

Sometimes I am not moving.
Sometimes, the tower spins
like a lighthouse beside me.

The Sky to the Ground

Apartments and shops
spread to the curb,
rubble of bricks and rebar,
hammered with a yellow,
steal cat.

Many exchanges were locked in those walls:

Lunches spent in humid afternoons,
slow and tired evenings
staring onto the streets
absorbing the rumble of buses,
the air of shattering horns
honking their way through
the chaos of traffic.

Seems like water
how the building flows
to the road or into the backs
of dump trucks.

All those gatherings hauled away
to fill some hole
dug for stone or soil
for new walls stacked
higher and solidly frozen
to attach the sky to the ground.

Mandala

All points begin—there are no points of origin.
Wherever I arrive, I have begun.
I do not change. I have accrued a light density,
and I begin from where I had begun
and where I had arrived at my conclusions.

I orbit inside the sphere, in lines and curves,
pushed or acting, both subject and object,
in any direction, knocked in another by a force
or by choice of given choices either random
or amassed, either by cause or by effect—
all stops like spheres in motion,
my thoughts, ideas, my blood and breath,
like water clicking off rounded corners, pushing
and being pushed, in an ordered turbulence
inside an expansion,
a borderless mandala—
no surface except the surface of motion.

The Water of Joy

The chanting at Ānguó Sì
reaches deeply into timelessness,
foregoes a need for understanding.

Small white butterflies
float above tiny magenta flowers
the size of fingerprints.

I am in between me and not me.
I am not a father; I am a father.
I am not a husband; I am a husband.
I am not me; I am me.

No reason in a heart beat
of an old human chant without time,
without development of time—

The heartbeat of the soul,
of energy, of voice—

The keeper of the mind is the heart,
the silencer of reason.

The mantra pulls from the deep
well of sorrow to drink
the water of joy.

Wild Tea

We drink hot
wild green tea
and Ruta Maya coffee
in a shop of silk dresses.

Om Mane Padme Om
plays on the speaker
deep in China.

Good friends speak
Chinese to me.
I am part of the group,
and I understand not a word.

The effort to understand
                        drops away.

Simple joy lightly smiles.

Serentiy Whispers

Like whispers,
the silence of serenity
surrounds the shell of noise
my mind hides within.

Peace may leak
through the cracks in the air

to the natural stillness
like the bitter green sprout
curled in a white lotus seed.

To See in Autumn

Sometimes, the nectar of the mind,
like slowly flowing illustrious amber,
bends the light like an Autumn's noon
calm and yellow, a translucent eyeball
sliding across the days and down the trees
absorbing everything and holding on to nothing,
lightly striving to forget itself like water.

Sometimes, the sun stalks the mind
lighting up everything with powerful whispers
about expanding behind the sunset.

Sometimes, the mind might stop trying
to see inside the sunset and blink
for a moment one breath long
like waking from a dream of Fall
to see a red leaf carried gently by the wind.

A Shade of Purple Each River Mile

When I develop a cold
that wants, if it has a desire,
to slide down my throat and play
in my lungs, where it can make families
that could eventually strike out on their own
with a powerful sneeze, I feel doomed,
for those little bugs bounce on my nerve endings
which send low frequency signals to my mood,
which controls the definition of reality.

But, interestingly enough, a simple ride,
like being on a cheap kayak and lifting the oar
to let the current turn me around and around
at its whim, like a light sleep with easy breathing,
stays the struggle to maintain the quality
of the substance produced from the source of the cold—

As if today and yesterday and perhaps tomorrow, too,
were shaped by signals from an insignificant source
so powerful to construct a mock reality
replete with mass and height and measurable qualities—

So that I might sit and breathe, take up the oar,
the atoms in the walls would part,
and I could watch how each swooping martin
swiftly flying by a few inches above the water
gradually changes shades of violet
on its wings with each river mile.

The Question of the Breeze
for Content

Let me say that I have lost
a few pounds in sweat alone.

There either was a breeze,
or there was not a breeze.

With the heat coming from above
and from below, radiating from the concrete,

and added the magnificence of walking
across a bridge like this one,

pausing to look onto the rice fields,
across the tops of flowers and a stream

to a mountain across the valley,
I see the field full of green is enough

to cancel one's desire for a breeze.

Loud Song!

The tree frogs must think
their song of the forest

is more important
than my deepest thoughts!

I Caught a Fly

I had washed my hands
and had not dried them.

A fly sought water or a crumb
along the rim of a silver metal soup pot.

My hand acted more swiftly
than I could have commanded.

Wings tickled my palm
inside my gently closed fist.

"Come outside with me and see,"
I told my wife. "Watch it fly away."

I noticed its shimmer on its eyes,
slightly metallic, when it fell to the porch.

"Quickly! Dry your wings," I said.
"Birds like to come here and eat bread crumbs!"

Its hind legs brushed the backs of its wings
between each set of fanning them.

"Hurry!" I said. "Dry your wings and fly!"
I slowly moved my index finger closer.

"There it goes," I told my wife
when the fly jolted into the dusk light.

"You should not eat chicken," said my wife.
"You should not eat pork. You should eat vegetables."

We returned to the kitchen
where I sliced colorful small peppers for dinner.

Mahamudra Pancakes

The pancakes soak in their self-pools of syrup,
slathered in melting minds of butter.
We sit, in twos or more, with pairs of eyes
wider than the widest cake, seeing not the pancakes,
but the world of the pancakes and the silent
understanding of the universe that brought them there:
the waiter who works a smile into work,
the hairnets on the capped cooks
who sweat above the frying pans,
the underpaid manager ordering bulk food
to put pennies in a jar, the strands of hair
slipping into the young woman's eye
as she spends her body's motion over a griddle,
the pipes under the foundation
that guide the gas to fuel the flames
to raise the dough,
the day turned night enough
to begin another round of breakfast,
a patch of neon reds and greens
reflected off the kitchy table tops,
the cups of cooling coffee poured too late at night
to warrant any excuse not to have another,
and the endless hum of blurred conversations
with no discernable words,
but with a single-pathed, one-minded
shifting of emotional meaning,
then we, the two or more or the two of us,
can un-mind our minds and eat
the pancakes that were never there
except for in the context of the pancake world.

Zen—

Between something and the nothing that is also something—

where bells ring when the red lights on the radio towers blink;
where colors like thick, fresh bread fill the drafts—
when a snake darts into the back door and a child yells, "Snake!"

—between the fragrance of the wet grass after the sprinkler is turned off,
and the texture like a creek's stone when the wind bends
the autumn light and sets it on the morning glory's leaves
and its red bean seeds—

within the coolness in the backyard's soft breathing,
the mocking bird's arpeggio, the yellowing questions
ready to slide down columns of the breeze
and slip into hibernating silence, soil brown—

when the night rises, slick like a clean, dark robe,
in a cat's eye, one green, one yellow,
both opening to catch a glimpse of quiet owls—
both eyes listening to feathered songs of hushing streets,
porchlights' ambers, silent stories inside brick siding—

— tensions weave day masks and hang them above the couch,
and owl feathers glide purple silence into kitchens and bedrooms.

One Year of Breaths

Partnered air and water—
when I breathe
Autumn after dusk,

when I lift one foot
and the other is down,
is walking a partnership
of up down backward and forward?

If I breathe in during the night
when the air is cold in Autumn,
do I merge like partners
with the warmth from my outbreath?

Who I am today
one year after my father's death?
Partners with the absence?

One breath a sunset.
One breath a sunrise.
No partner with an hour or a year.
One moment in between.

From Sunshine's Eye

The tower casts a calm peace
across samsara like a lighthouse
sending a beacon over rocks and waves,

beckoning the lost in the darkness
to come and taste natural serenity.

The tower holds a tree
above the constructs
built by busy minds

to emanate peace,
the mind's natural state.

For peace to grow,
there must be breath,
there must be kind action.

For the tree to grow,
there must be water.

A firetruck sends water
high enough for the tree
atop Qīng Yún Tǎ at Ānguó Sì.

The water arches like a rainbow,
then rains like a waterfall
down the bricks to the foundation.

Nature sprouts new leaves
atop the beacon of peace.

Today's Blossom

I can't claim to know
how to hold onto kindness,
but today blossoms.

Blossoms on the Pavement

There are flowers
even in the rain
at night when our feet
are wet and we feel
overlooked by the day.

They come up like little
explosions on the dark
pavement, white
in the beams of headlights.

They give us no choice
except to grab our attention
and snatch us away
from our useless thoughts
with their subtle
short bursts of petals.

Crazy Beauty

Such crazy beauty in a red-eye flower
cut and blooming in a dusty vase
next to a sink of unwashed dishes that stink.

The red paints the backs of my eyes
sloppily, clumsily, thickly.

So raw, the red, that the skin over my mind burns,
leaving thoughts opened and vulnerable.

Furiously Tiny

What happened to the pink flower,
furiously tiny, that stopped time,
so striking above the grass blades
yesterday morning before I shut
the car door to begin my drive to work?

The Flowers Have Violet Wings

The bee and the flower
seem different.
The flower radiates a color
it cannot see.
The bee feeds on the flower
enticed by the offering.

The connection casts invisibility
onto the participants,
so their separateness prevails
as identity.

Does the veil obscure
the view so that all the eye sees
filters through a pinhole
the size of a pupil?

If so, an observer could easily
form an identity separate from
others, like the colors of flowers
or the wings on the bees.

Or does the invisible shade one's
color from one's self, like the flower
that has no eye to use to decide
between magenta or violet?

The link between the resonance
of one's self and the connection
to the receptor could hide,
and separateness would prevail.

A poet lived a long time ago
in China, and one day he talked
with a magistrate who told him
a fable he had not heard.

The magistrate said
that a bird and a bat
met to discuss which
meant daytime.

The bat said daytime begins
when the sun goes down,
and the bird said daytime starts
when the sun rises.

The poet whistled and sang
a song of being in between
the dusk and the sunrise,
and in the chorus he sang
that neither the bird nor the bat
could see that day and night
do not oppose one another,
that they express the same song
about the light.

The bee and the flower
form two organs of the same
body of light. Which one would
exist if the other could not?

To behave as a flower
and express the light by color,
the other must receive the frequency
to sustain itself.

We reflect so many frequencies
that our receptors break them into static.
We sing like birds of daylight,
or we send our high-pitched,
sonic beams into the night,
separate from the day,
with the form of wings
and a shape of dark blue.

All the shapes and colors of flight
combine, though, like organs
in a body made of light.

There Is Tea

I sit like a temporary neighbor
to the clouds, as if it is natural,
as if the metal wings
are mine.

I do not notice, though.
Like walking, I do not always
think feet, feet, feet.

It is too easy to eat rice
at six hundred miles per hour
and forget I sit
in the belly
of the sky.

Earth passes passively
underneath, not hurried
to bear the changes
hands and feet
scratch in its face.

I leave one home,
I speed to the second,
and in between
there is tea.

Circles Never End

We completed a circle,
first as strangers
from opposite sides of the earth,
climbing an old tower
whose steps are worn smooth
by thousands of meetings like ours.

We struggled to merge our languages,
finding similarities at each step,
reaching a view of a long river
under a miraculous tree!

How funny fate can be!

How it reunites family
across a sea,
across a culture,
across a language,
across time,
across no space at all!

We climbed the stairs again
with added family
when it was time to depart,
seeking a stone
with the words on it
we carved in our past lives.

There is no beginning.
There was no departure.

The statues and the stones
chip and fade.

The flower lamps softly burn.
We will always refill the oil.

CPSIA information can be obtained
at www.ICGtesting.com
Printed in the USA
BVHW030850070620
581005BV00002B/524